curious about

SEARCH AND RESCUE DOGS

BY CARI MEISTER

AMICUS LEARNING

What are you

curious about?

Curious About is published by
Amicus Learning, an imprint of Amicus
P.O. Box 227, Mankato, MN 56002
www.amicuspublishing.us

Editor: Ana Brauer
Series Designer: Kathleen Petelinsek
Book Designer and Photo Researcher: Sara Hood

Cataloging-in-Publication data is available
from the Library of Congress.
Library Binding ISBN: 9798892008563
Paperback ISBN: 9798892009225
eBook ISBN: 9798892009881
LCCN: 2025012833

Photo Credits: Alamy Stock Photo/dpa, cover, 1, Dubois/Andia,
18–19, Jim Holden, 15, Penny Kendall, 3, 17; Getty Images/
Andreas Arnold/picture alliance, 12–13, FABRICE COFFRINI,
2, 6, Ibrahim Yozoglu/Anadolu, 11, Peter Kneffel/picture
alliance, 9, TerryJ, 4–5, THOMAS SAMSON, 10; Shutterstock/
cynoclub, 7 (bottom), E LLL, 7 (top), Eric Isselee, 7 (second
from top), Mary Swift, 7 (middle), Nejron Photo, 7 (second
from bottom), Noska Photo, 2, 14, Stoyan Yotov, 20–21; The
Noun Project/Andi Nur Abdillah, 22, 23, Iconic, 22, 23

Every effort has been made to contact copyright holders for
material reproduced in this book. Any omissions will be rectified
in subsequent printings if notice is given to the publisher.

1

What is a search and rescue dog?

A dog that finds lost people! When someone is missing or there's been a **disaster**, search and rescue (SAR) dogs go to work. They use their noses to find people who need help.

Search and rescue dogs are trained to look for people in danger.

What kinds of dogs become search and rescue dogs?

Saint Bernards are popular SAR dogs.

Many different kinds! Any medium-sized dog who loves to learn can become a SAR dog. Labs, golden retrievers, and border collies make good searchers. They are smart, strong, and love to work. SAR dogs help scared people. So, they also need to be very friendly.

BLOODHOUND

BASSET HOUND

COONHOUND

BEAGLE

SAINT BERNARD

How do the dogs find people?

Some SAR dogs follow footprints and clues on the ground. Other dogs sniff the air to catch **scents**. These dogs can smell someone buried under snow, mud, or **rubble**. They can find people up to 15 feet (4.6 meters) under the ground.

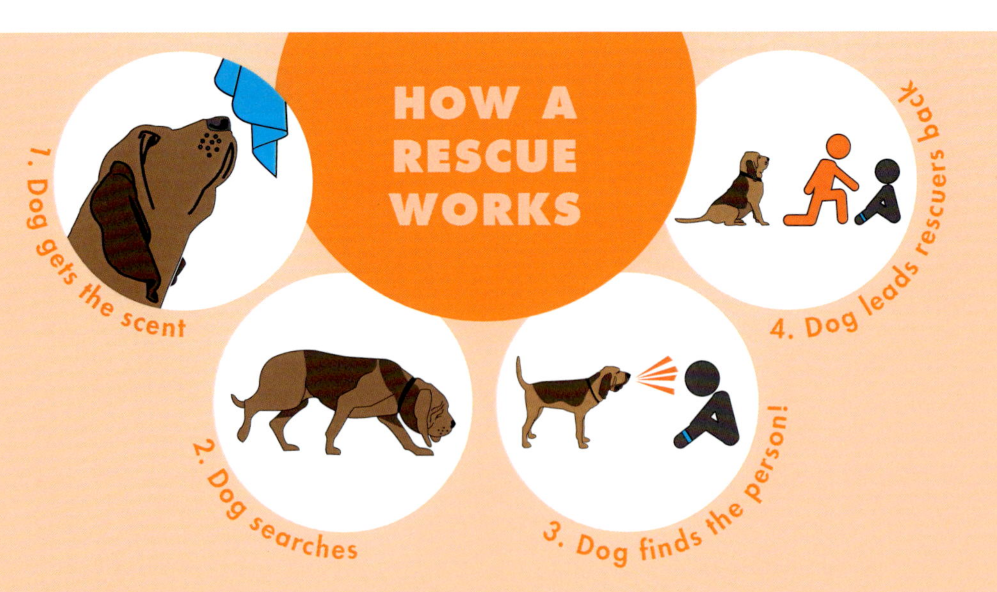

**DID
YOU KNOW?**
A SAR dog can
cover more ground in 30
minutes than four people
searching for two hours.

How do rescue dogs learn their job?

Training starts as a fun game. The trainers hide. Then the dogs find them! The dogs get treats when they are quick. SAR dogs learn to work in all kinds of places. They even practice searching in the dark.

SAR dogs start learning with games like hide-and-seek.

SAR dogs also learn how to find people in the water.

How long does training take?

About two years! SAR dogs start with simple games. Then they learn harder skills like searching in bad weather and working at night. Some SAR dogs start as puppies. Others learn when they are grown.

What happens when they find someone?

These dogs know just what to do! Some stay right next to the person they find and bark for help. Others are messengers. When they find a person, they run back to their handlers. Then, they lead their handlers back to the person who needs help.

This SAR dog leads its handler to a person in need.

DID YOU KNOW? Every minute counts in a rescue. SAR dogs must work as fast as they can. Finding people quickly saves lives.

Where do search and rescue dogs work?

All over the world! They search in forests when hikers get lost. They look through fallen buildings after storms. Some work in snowy mountains to find people buried in **avalanches**. Some of these brave dogs will dig through snow to help free people who are trapped.

A SAR dog can smell someone buried deep under snow.

How do rescue dogs help in disasters?

This SAR dog sniffs earthquake rubble to find anyone who might be trapped or hurt.

When big storms or earthquakes happen, rescue dogs rush to help! Their amazing noses can find people trapped under buildings or mud. They dig and bark. They often work day and night helping bring people to safety.

What makes rescue dogs special?

SAR dogs work hard to save people. They often put their own lives in danger. They climb over fallen buildings. They work in deep, unsafe snow. They search hot, dry deserts and steep mountain cliffs. They are real-life heroes!

DID YOU KNOW?
Even heroes need breaks! Between rescues, SAR dogs play with toys, go for walks, and spend time with their families.

Avalanche dogs and other SAR dogs work with their handlers as a team.

ASK MORE QUESTIONS

What do rescue dogs do when they're not working?

Could my dog become a SAR dog?

Try a BIG QUESTION: Why are dogs better at finding people than machines?

SEARCH FOR ANSWERS

Search the library catalog or the Internet.
A librarian, teacher, or parent can help you.

Using Keywords
Find the looking glass.

Keywords are the most important words in your question.

?

If you want to know about:

- SAR dog training, type: SEARCH AND RESCUE DOG TRAINING

- rescues in your area, type: SEARCH AND RESCUE DOGS [YOUR STATE]

FIND GOOD SOURCES

Here are some good, safe sources you can use in your research.
Your librarian can help you find more.

Books

Jobs of a Working Dog: Search and Rescue Dogs
by B. Keith Davidson, 2022.

Search and Rescue Dogs
by Marie Brandle, 2022.

Internet Sites

American Rescue Dog Association
https://www.ardainc.org
This group trains rescue dogs and shares real stories about their work.

National Search and Rescue Dog Association Kids Page
https://www.nsarda.org/kids
This site is made just for kids to learn about rescue dogs and their work.

Every effort has been made to ensure that these websites are appropriate for children. However, because of the nature of the Internet, it is impossible to guarantee that these sites will remain active indefinitely or that their contents will not be altered.

SHARE AND TAKE ACTION

With an adult, watch a search and rescue dog demonstration in your community.
Many teams do shows at schools and fairs.

Make thank-you cards for your local search and rescue dog teams.

Learn about outdoor safety so SAR dogs won't need to find you!

GLOSSARY

avalanche A big amount of snow sliding down a mountain.

disaster A sudden event causing much damage or suffering.

handler The person who works with and cares for a rescue dog.

rubble Broken pieces of a destroyed building.

scent The smell a person or animal leaves behind and a dog can follow.

INDEX

About the Author

Cari Meister has written many books for children about dogs. She recently rescued a Great Dane puppy from an animal shelter. Cari loves learning about how dogs help keep communities safe. She lives in Vail, Colorado, and sees avalanche dogs at work all winter long.